ABOUT THE AUTHOR

Rupinder Kaur is a Birmingham born Panjabi poet with an immense love for South Asian arts. She sees writing and reading poetry as a way to liberate the soul. This is her first collection.

Twitter: @rupinderkw
Instagram: @rupinderkw_
Facebook: https://www.facebook.com/rupinderkaurw/
Website: rupinderkw.com

Rupinder Kaur

Rooh

VERVE
POETRY PRESS
BIRMINGHAM

PUBLISHED BY VERVE POETRY PRESS
Birmingham, West Midlands, UK
www.vervepoetrypress.com
mail@vervepoetrypress.com

FIRST PUBLISHED SEPT 2018
REPRINTED MAY 2019

Printed and bound in the UK
by Imprint Digital, Exeter

ISBN: 978-1-912565-08-5

Cover art by Maryam Mughal
Facebook: https://www.facebook.com/MughalART/
Peacock feather art by Derya Rasit
Instagram: derya141

aufIk qyrI rUh nUM
udeek teri rooh nu
my soul waits for you

Art, poetry, writing; where does any creative expression come from? I remember quite clearly the first time I fell in love with the Panjabi language, listening to a Qawwali sung by Nusrat Fateh Ali Khan. The Qawwali, originally penned by Shiv Kumar Batalvi, a well renowned Panjabi poet who I now consider to be my favourite, began as a poem: "Maye ni maye, mere geetaan de naina vich birhon di rarak pavey." The Qawwali transported me to another world and inspired me to begin exploring poetry. It was during this journey that I first came across Amrita Pritam, a female Panjabi poet known for her famous piece calling upon Waris Shah, the greatest poet in the history of Panjab. I feel that it was through Amrita's words that I truly began to find myself.

People often say to me "You must have been born in Panjab, to have such a love towards your mother tongue!" In fact, it wasn't until I was nineteen that I learned how to read and write the language. These days I spend as much time as I can to read Panjabi poetry to understand my mother's words.

At a time when many children of the Asian diaspora are losing touch with their mother tongues, others are finding them through poetry and through music. Today there is a real sense of reclaiming our cultural identity and heritage. Unlike our first-generation parents, we are now rediscovering our voices and telling our histories through the medium our ancestors once favoured – through poetry. I'm grateful to my mother for telling me stories while putting me to sleep. From the love tales of Sohni and Mahiwal, Heer and Ranjha to the Udasis of Guru Nanak Dev Ji, the influence of these stories now heavily shapes and inspires my own poetry. The folk tales our grandmothers sang at weddings and the tales of bravery recited to awestruck children were all brought to life in the very same way.

The beauty of language is that it is 'azaad,' – free from borders, independent of nationality and state. The language you love you love becomes yours, it becomes your home, your country.

Our 'Rooh,' our pure and true soul (where I feel expression itself is born,) is fluent. The words have always been inside, lying dormant, waiting for us to pick up a pen and spill the ink across the paper, to give them new life.

My Rooh is a journey through which I transcend borders and rivers. Poetry is my mode of transport.

Rupinder 2019.

Rooh

rUh | Rooh

A word which unties Panjabi, Hindi, Urdu, Arabic and Persian
meaning soul.

The soul sees no religion. The soul sees no border. The soul is free.

From the ruins of an Masjid
to the streets of Delhi
to a room where old songs are playing
Urdu- Hindi- Panjabi fuses
to the remains of a Mandir
searching for the beauty of a different century
walking across Amritsar
wanting the purity of raags
with the words of Guru Nanak
leaving it amrit thirsty
for another time.
And it hears the flute of Krishna
and dances just like a Gopi,
traveling to another time,
sitting with Sufis at the dargah,
hearing the kalam of Bulleh Shah.
It travels through space and time
coming alive in a new body,
hearing the voice of Nusrat
and the poetry of Shiv Kumar Batalvi.
And somewhere between time's beginning and end

it wanders and travels
between countries
across oceans
landing in Birmingham,
lost somewhere
and found somewhere
in the chaste of Panjab.

　　　　　　　　　－ rooh, soul.

****

Delhi
the home of Ghalib
and my mother's city –
Delhi
the lanes of Chaukhandi,
where Mandirs, Masjids and Gurdwaras
are at the same distance
with colourful bazaars at each corner.
Mother says the best days were spent buying dolls
and eating chole bhature
and the best time of the year
was when classes would change
and fresh new notebooks would be given.
Mother says the best thing about school was
drying the takhti, the mud slates.
While they would dry she would sing Bollywood songs
with her friends
and they would shake their hips like Sridevi
trying to do the naagin dance.
Thrn coming home and climbing to the rooftops,

trying to see Qutub Minar,
with evenings spent watching Vikram aur Betaal.
There was always a light problem
but there was so much happiness in little things
from buying cycles to washing machines.
It all meant so much...

She turned thirteen
and crossed to a whole new world by aeroplane,
from Delhi to Birmingham.

****

I am carrying the lines of borders in my veins and arteries.
My chromosomes carry the sex of partition.
I cross borders in my body
to become my own country.

I carry tramua inside my DNA -
years of searching
years of finding.
I am the generation after parting
yet I do not truly know what it means
to have to leave your home

every night –
I hear the sounds of sitars and tablas in my dreams.
I hear the sounds of anklets with silhouettes swaying.
I see swords making love to pens
with lovers uniting at dusk while waves meet the moon.
With snakes hissing and tigers roaring

the monsoon comes, and the peacocks dance,
and my hands become stained with mendhi.
Each night, the fragrance of some place comes and wakens me.

This foreign land is not my home
but perhaps the ocean in-between
that I pass to reach home
in my dreams
is my home.
Maybe that is where I am not foreign
and I am just right.
To be there and here...
maybe that is my home...

****

Forever missing my train
just by a second
and forever at every bookshop
going to all the local libraries
searching for names of authors that look like mine
with some English Panjabi Hindi Urdu -
Bombay mixture writing like mine
stuck in this
colonial and postcolonial
literature of absence
longing for that back home essence.

Searching between lines
searching for the truth
I am forever searching....
         I am forever searching...

****

poetry
[poh-i-tree]
(noun) art of rhythmical composition, written or spoken.

Not just English literature
nor the works of dead men.
Poetry is the art of women too.
Poetry is the art of black and brown too.
Poetry is living and breathing every day.
Poetry is the way my people live.
Poetry is the way my people pray...

Years of slavery and colonisation
led us to bite our own tongues
and forget that poetry runs in our blood.
Poetry is our liberation
and poetry is our power.

****

waqt ne meri kalam phar lai
hath sade khali ho gaye
zuba sadi band ho gayi

Time has taken my pen away.
Our hands are empty,
our mouths are closed ...

Everyone's mouths are closed. They don't speak., they don't talk
and no one is writing/

Perhaps I should eat a dictionary for breakfast
and a thesaurus for dinner. Perhaps then words will reappear.
And I will find the correct words inside me
And be able to write about God like philosophers

Maybe everyone should eat a dictionary for breakfast
and ta hesaurus for dinner.
Then everyone will realise the power of words

Right now I see a river of words
dissolving into the west horizon...
The tide of time floats away.
My kalam comes back into my hands
and maybe it will come back into everyone's hands too.

****

Challa

Across oceans
          to my bedroom
entering my heart
the challa comes.

The challa starts searching
but finds my heart
                  full of words
in displaced languages.

The challa doesn't fit
          but the challa sits

waking me up from a deep sleep
so that I see everything so differently
like I had been asleep for so long.

But instead of the future
it's like I have gone back in time
finding the words of my grandmother inside me
         finding words of a lost language inside me
speaking challa, challa.

Challa the word, meaning ring sometimes
meaning mad sometimes
and sometimes meaning someone, searching...

Challa.

The challa sits inside my heart perfectly
watching me fall in love,
watching me speak the language of my heart
so beautifully...

Challa.

****

I am the winds of Lahore
that my Nanaji brought
across the border of Wagah.

I am the soil of Amritsar
where my father was born.

I am mixed with the air coming from Delhi
where my mother was born.

Who am I?
is a question I am yet to solve.
I am divided into names and culture.
I sit oceans away from Panjab
yet I write about Panjab.

I am somewhat British
yet more Panjabi.
I write in English
wishing I wrote more in Panjabi...

****

My grammar, my English
have never   been very good

I've been learning   to balance languages
on the tip   of my tongue
since I was born.
While mixing   between my mother tongues
my English   often breaks
in places.
      I fall short   of English
and that's when I   remember my mother tongue.
   But sometimes   all I have is English
and sometimes I only   have my mother tongue to cry in.

****

asa chal gaye pardas
te sadi boli rul di pai

we have gone abroad
and our language is in ruins

****

I lost my mother
in pages of history,
in pages of literature.
I lost my mother

when I learnt a b c before a A e.
(oora aara eeri)
I lost my mother
in diluted pages of translations.

She can't be translated -
she is too pure.
She is too pure.
But people never understood that
so I lost her.

And I lost her again
while writing this...

****

zuban ka nahi koi dharam
yeh toh azaad hai
yeh sarahado se paar hai

The tongue has no religion.
It is free
It is beyond borders

****

Ghalib's kitaab
sits on the doorstep of my mother's old home.
It travels across borders
and in through my window.
It rowses me from my sleep
so I read and read.

Shiv Kumar Batalvi's kitaab
dances by the river Ravi,
comes to the river Thames
and then a few miles further.
It too enters my room
through the open window.

Urdu and Panjabi words
spin around in my room
looking at each other
saying: kya baath, kya baath
asi rubaro, asi rubaro
we are rubaro! – wow
we are face to face...

The words laugh at each other
thinking of the irony –
how they are brought together in England
and into English are translated,
how they meet on the lips of lovers
and how they merge into the ocean of language.
How funny to see
how some understand them better than others
and how some don't even want to know them.

John Keats and Blake are watching
as Urdu and Panjabi meet
oceans away from their homes.
And Ghalib and Shiv meet
in the same century, at the same time
sitting together in my bookcase...

****

Aunty Ji from down the road
comes with her dosa diaries
mixing with the air coming from the south
to our Panjabi tarka house.

It's Diwali
and aunty Amar comes and gives us a box of jalebis.
Lights are lit in every brown house on the road.

The house in front of us has cool white kids
who play in the road
while I play in my back garden.

We know it's Eid
when our next door neighbours
bring flashy cars to B21.
Mum wishes Eid Mubarak to them

The newlywed nineteen year old Preeti
fresh from Panjab
comes and invites us to dinner.
mum says we'll see if we get time.

As I do my maths homework
mum reads Gurbani.

And now it's 3 pm.
I wanna watch Bhaji on the Beach
but mum tells me to get some onions
so I walk to the corner shop.
Finally, it's time to eat.
I eat my favourite rajma chawal...

And years later I still love my mum's rajma chawal
missing the ends of B21,
missing my old home on Wattvile Road.

****

Born in the ghetto
coming from the gully, the road
straight from the gully
yes ghetto di kudi.

Handsworth raised -
and yes my ends are rough
yes my ends are tough -
but B21 gotta represent.
My Nanaji set foot here back in the 70's.
The home of Browns and Blacks.
The home of minority communities.

Communities leeching off colonialism/
Handsworth revolution,
but that's a story for another day.
we got Benjamin Zephaniah
spitting bare bars of truth,
apache Indian givin dem reggae vibes and Indian sounds.
The sounds of B21 smashing it throughout.

I listen to grime, to sufi,
with some Panjabi and Hindi,
to abit of r&b.
Gone are my Paramore days -
now its all about fusing the qawwali

from Wattville Road to Holyhead road.
I see some Polish and Somali families walk by.
I see a bit of Pakistan, India and Bangaldesh
like pre-partition... come by

Down the police station
to the gurdwarda,
binds with jeans.
who do I think I am,

reading Bukowski and Batalvi
on the 74 bus
coming down to Soho Road ends
sada mini Panjab
the glory of my ends
the fame of Handsworth
sada Soho Road, our Soho Road
I will always be a handsworth gyal
yes ghetto di kudi. ////

****

The canals by Brindley place
become a prayer for Jhelum.

The library becomes a home for
reading Faiz and Iqbal
                    with Lahore coming so close
yet so far away.
            I write half ghazals
thinking of Amritsar and Delhi,
            languages spin intermingling
Hindi Panjabi Urdu English.
                    Which is mine?/ when all four are mine...

****

The qawwali is playing;
the tram is full
and sitting next to me,
is someone reading while I'm typing.

Pushchairs and bags are everywhere.
People cling to each other
like the flats of Bombay.

I travel from Patiala to Peshawar
sitting in a room in Prague
watching the sunset in Paris
from the smell of people
from the faces of people
unfamiliar but familiar.

I start thinking about this pre Brexit
wondering about post Brexit.

I am a child of immigrants
wondering if the sacrifice made
to leave home was worth it...

****

Layers of identity
        layers of names.
Which ethnic box do I tick?
        Am I British
                    or am I British Asian?
                        Or am I neither?
Who am I ?
My tongue doesn't realise when it changes from English
        to Panjabi   to Hindi   to Urdu
    or to something in-between
                    mixing everything
a perfect fit for fusion   maybe?

I sit watching more Bollywood than Hollywood
    with some Pollywood
Years of fighting with my brown dusky skin
    which   now   seems   so   cool....
but it's more than reclaiming clothes –
        how do you reclaim an identity?
my British tongue can't pronounce the Gurmukhi letter V
my own laugh at me for wanting to be like them back home....
BBCD?
they don't realise what displaced children suffer   layers
of identity
we the children of the diaspora   are in search of our roots, in
search of our true identity...
in search of our rooh
names and names is what get given   BAME. POC.
no one truly understands us not even our own   we
blame colonialism
we read books that aren't told about in school, we read about
our heroes that are never mentioned in school   but we hide
away the curry stains on our white shirts
we spray away the tarka smell   we get given fair and
lovely by our own
we hide everything   we hide our pain   because that's all
we have been taught
  we hide away   we hide away
but our brown skin wants to break   from layers and
layers
but   our lives are a dual identity   sometimes the
British-ness takes over and sometimes my rooh takes over.

****

kitaab-e-dil mein aarzoo ke fasaane
tumhare dard ke saath guzare zamaane
jaise mehfill mein bikhre afsaane

the book of my heart contains stories of desires
with your pain they have passed eras
just like gatherings with scattered tales

****

many words
many poems
many stories –

are unsaid
and silenced away;

inside the body
inside the soul
inside the heart –
of a woman.

****

Last night, I lay in bed
wishing to go back in time,
to be that young girl once again
that would dance in the rain
wearing my mother's suits,
wearing her bangles with her high heels
that were too big for me then.

I lay remembering when my brother was born
and the moment I held him in my arms.
I always knew he would be special.
Dad was always busy working,
doing it for the family,
mother doing her thing,
being the good mother and wife...
I remember a few days ago mother told me
when I was younger I was a cheeky girl
that always answered back
and wouldn't take no for answer.
I remember that moment
when I crossed the path -
from a young girl to a woman -
in one night.
I became mature too soon.
My body ripened too soon.
I became a woman too soon
and lost my innocent self too soon.
I didn't realise now my no meant yes...
and that the curves of my body
had become a sin,
that I had become a captive
inside the walls of my own body.

****

I wanted to tell you how I felt
but words got stuck in my throat
I left them in the windows of my eyes...
                    while playing my favourite song –

dil cheez kya hai?
app meri jaan liyiye –
why just my heart?
take my whole life too...

****

Sins make their way into my body before praying.
Shame dances shamelessly in my soul.
Sex tells me I am desired.
A sinister is what I have become.
Sawan comes
so raags play
sa re ga ma pa
sa re ga ma pa
Satisfying my body
so sarcastically hidden,
sealing the doors of my heart.
Superstition is still alive.
So smoothly he comes,
selfish pleasures, with mine forgotten...
Silk sheets move away
so I sleep away
so I sleep away....
Sometimes I forget *havaas ishq nahi* (lust is not love)/
nor an escape.

****

A silent night it was,
with desires of passion
neither sweet nor sour
- just a silent night.

Skin was passing over skin.
The candle was burning -
so was I...
The fire of lust passed over time
and I sacrificed a piece of myself,
not to God...
but to you.

Breathless moments
filled with fake ecstasy,
speaking of Divinity,
while misogyny danced
on the curves of my body
running away from stops of capitalism,
leeching off feminism.
Celibacy must be a good joke.
Even virgins are laughing
in this right-wing world.

You came as a God to my bed
and left as an atheist
careless, necking,
I – a sacred sight
draped in a fake shrine.
I was a Goddess
dressed in white.

but I became a sinister
the moment I bled
and the angels sang away.
Apollo missed his strike,
Venus sat between my legs
with love and lust mixed away
love and lust mixed away.
A silent night it was...

****

wafa ki baate karte karte
hum toh khud bewafa nikle

talking and talking of being faithful
I became a betrayer myself.

****

I have been touched in ways
I can't tell anyone about
and I have sins I can't tell God about.
I try to find God inside me
but I fail.
I try and pray
but my mind goes into flashback mode.
I have wounds on my skin that don't show.
I always think the worst -
that I will fail every test -
and my nerves always take over
so my mind shuts off
and I can't hear anything

apart from my own loud heartbeat.
I get told I'm too emotional
and therapists tell me time will heal me.
They say I am just paranoid
because everyone I loved in the past...left
and the men I encounter just make it worse.
So I break my own heart
by leaving before they do
and never committing....
Younger me lashed out on my wrists
making them bleed blood.
Now my blood bleeds ink
making me write poetry
becoming my liberation
and prayer.
I exist because of poetry.
          Tell me to stop writing
          and I will die.

****

You touched my ijsm – body
but you could never touch my rUh – soul...

– Jism and rooh; even though they exist
together
  they aren't one.

****

I wanted to see the dew drops
fall so beautifully forever
while wishing the flowers
would bloom forever.

Another day passes,
months pass by,
and years pass by,

I wanted to hold you
against my skin
and never let you go.

But the more I wanted you to stay
the more you went away.

And now I have to let you go.
I have to break my skin open.
to breathe in new air,
so I can bloom again.

****

Ba-dastoor – unaltered.
It makes no difference if you leave or go.
I am my own lover / I have found solace with my solitude.
I am mukammal, complete by myself .
I am in a state where neither sadness/ happiness affects me.
I am ba-dastoor, unaltered...I will remain as I am.
My eyes have seen so many faces of deceit,
lies told with hands on hearts,
relationships along with fake friendships.

I've seen it all
I have seen my own cheat and betray right in front of me.
So now I am ba-dastoor, unaltered.
Pain doesn't bother me anymore
I am ba-dastoor, unaltered.

****

I am jealous.
Yes, I am jealous
when I walk through the kabristan, the graveyard
by my house.

and I hear nothing but my own heartbeat
and I can feel my blood flowing through my veins
giving me a tingly feeling in my stomach
and I feel the most alive, knowing death is my reality...

The sukoon, the peace that I search for everyday,
the sukoon that I want from this world,
comes only when I walk through the kabristan.

I look at the flowers on the graves
with the odd poems engraved
and I smile
knowing one day
I will be gone too
and again I smile
knowing one day
my rooh will truly be azaad from my jism
and I shall be free from this duniya, this world.

I am jealous.
Yes, I am jealous
when I walk through the kabristan, the graveyard
by my house...
because it is only place that exists with complete sukoon, peace.

****

This is a poem for the time I saw my body's stretch marks as ugly.
But I already wrote this poem in my mother's womb.
This is my love poem.
This is a poem for when I was twelve and I hated my nose
so when I turned nineteen I got it pierced to make it stand out.
So now... no I'm not sorry that
my hooked long nose goes
against your eurocentric beauty standards.

And no, I'm not sorry that,
that my brown eyes aren't thought beautiful.
But I promise you you'll never see a pair of eyes like mine
that are big and wide - filled with the depth of the ocean

and no, no... I'm not sorry that,
I don't fit in with your perception of beauty.
I still don't see myself on any magazine covers
but now, I've become my own representation of brown.

Do my curves make you feel uncomfortable,
and my back and spine that hold so much strength and power?
No love, I'm not sorry
that I don't fit in with your idealisation of a perfect woman.

And does my brown skin make you feel uneasy?
Or that I have no truck with the 450 million dollar skin
        bleaching industry?
God painted me in golden rays of light
not to fit in with your fair-skinned beauty ideals
but to stand out...

darling... no, no, no I'm not apologetic.
                              I'm a brown woman
who's not defined by your eurocentric beauty standards...

****

I am removing decades of silence
and destroying cultural codes.
I am turning into Kali Ma
killing all the demons
and straining the coloniser out of my blood.
I am taking my own sex u ality back
holding it apart from exotic fascination.
I am telling you the erotic is power,
not just sexual but also spiritual.
My skin carries genocides.
I am too much skin.
My skin tells tales of a world of pre-colonised beauty.
Right now I am taking my own body back.
I am rewriting history.
Eve was born first, then Adam.
It is Shiv that needs Shakti.
My God comes as a woman
and now I am moving out of my territories,

away from my body's own borders,
turning into the ocean, flowing freely...

the young girl once a captive
in my body
is now azaad as a woman.

****

Main azaad ha
Main azaad parindey vang ha
I am free.
I am like free birds...

        I am free from rules.
I am free from the restraints of society.
            I am azaad, I am free.

I have broken every rule placed on my body.
        I have dared to
love myself.
I have crossed every line that has been drawn.
      I have resisted having strings attached.
I have gone past giving a fuck.
   I have broken
the norms of society
with the ink of my pen...

I have become the woman I always wanted to be –
I have become azaad, free.

Main azaad ha
Main azaad parindey vang ha
I am free
I am like free birds...

****

Metaphors and similes
can't describe her.

Metaphors and similes
can't tell what truth she holds.

She is not a fantasy.
Her body is not made for you to ride.

Her oxytocin
doesn't just get released when you touch her.

She isn't just
boobs and ass.

She isn't just
hymen
vagina
cervix
uterus
ovaries.

She is blood,
bones and magic.

She is not your Goddess.
She is her own God
and her body is her own temple
which certainly isn't yours to own.

Do not describe her like a poem.
She is not a poem.
She is beyond metaphors and similes.
she does not need your validation.

She is the creator
and she is the destroyer.
She is not art.

She is a woman,
not a flower.
She does not need metaphors and similes.
She is not a certain type.
She will not be tamed to your desires.

She is whole and not incomplete.
She is a woman
and not metaphors and similes...

****

what if I told you –
sometimes
I smoke   inhaling the air of patriarchal societies
to exhale the expectations of obedience and
                                        submissiveness

cause baby girls are unwanted
and some are killed in the womb
with some thrown away in rivers or buried back home
cause having a daughter is a somehow a curse...

So never pray for a daughter, only pray for a son
cause of this dowry traditional / cause of how girls bodies,
have been policed since they were born /cause of how society
sees girls/ girls don't carry the name forward / girls are forever
changing homes ,
if a girl makes one mistake the whole family is shamed
she is ghar ki izaat – the honour of the home ...
so watch what she wears, don't let her go out at night
watch who she speaks to ... make sure it's not someone of the
opposite gender
and make sure she's married off before 25 –
I never knew women were like food with expiry dates,
her best not to look over at me.

sometimes I wonder how did the word mistress-
go from meaning a woman having control and power
to the other woman?
                And you know exactly what I mean by that
and some will use the word feminist
as its some kind of abuse.
               They say you're just a male hating misandrist
but feminists wanna love too
and would too
if patriarchy...
homophobia
hypocrisy
and double standards
didn't get in the way.

Sometimes I wonder
how is sex linked with masculinity...
and somehow it is okay for a man to have sex before marriage
but somehow a woman having sex before marriage...
becomes a whore and impure right?
because virginity for a brown woman is sacred right?
only for your husband lord right?

And then there's all this emotional attyachar and drama
on izaat and sharam
feeding the male ego
with cultural dominance swinging by
with cultural traditional holding by
even if it kills women alive today.

Now I'm not about to blame anyone.
I know its a matter of chance what happens
but I'm stating what science tells me –
cause right now some mother-in-law is
screaming at her daughter-in-law for being infertile
not knowing that her son can also be infertile....
while some are right now crying about daughters
not knowing men carry the sex for having a boy.

We live in a world where a woman saying no –
could lead to getting raped or an acid attack
or being slut-shamed for the rest of her life
cause she hurt the macho man
for saying NO.

Marital rape is hidden away cause it's your husband
and its okay / you don't want to bring shame to your own
house/

I've lost count of the of the times I've seen bollywood songs
fantasize rape .
I've lost count of the times humanity has vanished.
I've lost count of the times I've heard women say it's love when
it's abuse.
I've lost count of the times I've seen sexual predators around
me.
I've lost count of the times I've seen women misused.
I've lost count of the times I've seen men lie to women
and women lying to men.
I've lost count of the times mothers have lied to children about
being happy.
I've lost count of the times cheating is accepted
and I've lost count of the times that   I've tried to love
men that   just wanna fuck me ...

I've worked hard to stand this tall
yet sometimes the touch of men makes me feel so weak
that I feel so small.
I wish I could enter an alternate world
where my 5ft 8 brown curvy body is not a sin
and my breasts are not wanted to be sucked for gratification.

but listen listen...
I don't wanna consume silence.
I wanna break the expectations placed on my body
my body is mine   my life is mine.

I get told I am too bold and I need to soften down
and marriage should be my end goal
and I shouldn't dream too much because I am a woman
and on top of that brown...

but I'm sure you gathered by now
I am not what I seem.
I am not a good typical satti satrvi brown girl
and I will continue to rebel against every rule that comes my way
because rules are made to be broken right?
so no I do not want to be a good brown girl...
no I do not want to be a good brown girl...

Hiding everything is all we seem to do / right...
These orthodox traditional lines of thought need to be changed.
The next generation of girls need to brought up in a society
where they can feel safe
and be azaad – free and not feel like they are ghar ki izaat.

****

away from orthodox ideologies
away from caste notions
along with rejecting satti and purdah
with female foeticide killers taken out
women taking arms
women at the front line of revolution

kOr
Kaur liberates me
Kaur frees me
Kaur taken by mother
Kaur taken my grandmother
Kaur taken by the women in my blood
rejecting social hierarchy
I am not bound to male patriarchy

name given to my tenth Guru –
Kaur.

****

This heart of mine it's so Kambakht
along with this ishq of mine
that's without any censorship...

So many tales spin around
this is air of mine. Kambakht world.
Woman body watches me as I break the rite of passage
making way for the thirst of men
but I am a wild horse that can't be tamed.
Sometimes I change midway into a sphinx
I have too many riddles....
somewhat of me is a mardaani
and sometimes I am too much woman
with too much fire –
I am a firefly that burns herself
writing herself alive.

My monogram is my mother's silence
but some try to silence me. Kambakht.

****

dear daughter –
men will try and crack your gaze
and tell you that your body is theirs to own
but remind them of how they were born from the door of
a woman /

Darling, caring too much and feeling too much
is not a problem
but when it begins to give pain   stop.
I know how it feels to give your everything
and receive nothing in return
I am used to it...
but I will never let you get used to being second best /

Society will tell you sex is dirty and a sin
but from this sin you are born.
Our culture holds centuries of shame for being a woman
and yes, if you break the silence
they will tell you, you are too bold
and outrageous.

Daugher, they will tell you that you can't fight
and that woman's place is not within the revolution
but remind them of Mai Bhago
and tell them of Gulab Kaur.
They will try censor your words
but remind them of Amrita Pritam

Dear daughter
remember to –
pick up a pen
pick up a paintbrush
do whatever
but do something that gives you the desire to live everyday/

and my dear daughter love with no boundaries
be free like the   wind flowing /

become the woman your mother could never be...

****

Putting my salwar on
I play Surinder Kaur's
ek meri akh kashni
written my favourite poet
Shiv Kumar Batalvi
that carries too much language
that can't be translated.
As I put my kameez on
it lines my body's curves
coming down with Lahore and Amritsar
a bit like my mother's salwar kameez
from an old photo
where she stands in-between
as she is the middle child
that has the worry of all.
The photo brings old Delhi where poetry lingers
and Sanskrit-Latin origin washes away -
no foeticide or qurbanis.
I remember my Nani Ji holding me,
calling me a ray of light – Kiran.
I see my Daadi ji looking at me
through the mirror smiling -
she lost her husband so young
yet she remained so strong
and raised two sons by herself
working hard day and night.
And as I place my dupatta by my side
I feel my ancestors next to me
traveling through two worlds
of life and death

coming at the platform of reality.
Feel too that I stand between two parallel lines
bringing a fusion of language
from every mohalla, area
that they set foot on from Lahore-Delhi-Amritsar
and finally Birmingham.

Yes, sometimes I write for myself
but mostly I write for my mother.
I write for my ancestors
that spill ink in every poem.

****

Walking from city to city
searching and searching
some say she's awari;
a vagrant, a wanderer;
her body is not her permeant home
let alone this world...

She dreams of hot Rajasthani winds
in the cities of dreams they say
but the desert of her own mind
is searching and searching...
for water
water from across oceans
from rivers, where lovers had their last breath
to quench her own rooh
but the water cannot be found.

She is a Banjaran
with no permeant home
her rooh is of a jogan, a female hermit
lost in this capitalistic world

Sbe is a migrant of this world
searching for earthly paak poetry, pure poetry
waiting for love –
a love like Shirin and Farhad
searching for the lover that will take her to firdaus, paradise.

She goes from one place to another
turning the wheel of time over and over
coming again and again
spending nights in lost cites
and now,
her eyes are smudged with kohl
with tales from every corner of the world
from snake charmers to cold London nights...

****

o mereya jugni, jugni
o mereya jugni, jugni

jugni travels from Delhi to Amritsar
across to England

jungi; the essence of life, the spirit of life
comes inside my rooh

jugni comes and dances in my dreams
jugni makes me fly

jugni takes me across borders
taking me to Lahore

jugni removes the radcliffe line
and I see my five rivers flowing together

jugni sees me read and write poetry
jugni tells me to light the candle

jugni watches me apply kohl
jugni watches me paint my lips

jugni looks at me and smiles
jugni tells me to fall in love with myself

jugni is no kafir or fakir
jugni is azaad, jugni is azaad

and jugni makes me free
jugni sets my rooh free

the jugni becomes me...
and the jugni becomes me...

o mereya jugni, jugni...
o mereya jugni, jugni...

****

some girls stand midway
                                    some girls look at me in the mirror
some girls are dripping in sweat
                                    some girls are washing off blood
some girls look happy but sad
                                            some girls apply kajal
some girls are taken away
                                        some girls are hidden away
some girls have broken bangles
                                    some girls are unmarried widows
some girls open their legs
                                            and are disgraced away
some girls are unmarried mothers
                                        some girls play their own flute
some girls watch their father lie
        some girls watch their mother die   some girls walk away
some girls become a living tomb
some girls slice their body   some girls sound like farsi
some girls are tired
                    some girls are fighting   some girls are crying
some girls are falling in love
                                    some girls are getting heartbreaks
some girls are doing gidha
                                        and spinning the charka
some girls stand between border lines
                            and   some girls are the border
some girls are flying kites
                        some girls are holding the Kalashnikov
and some girls are like the verses of poetry.

****

rishton ki zanjeeron mein bandhi aurat
azaadi ki khuwaahish mein jiye ja rahi hai

in the chains of relationships,
tied women live, wishing of freedom

****

The hairs in their eyebrows so thick, so dark
and their dusky brown skin glows
                like the waters of Ravi.
Their hair flows,
their dark black hair,
                like the colour of the soil.
Flowers must bloom through their soul.

Their eyes, shaped like almonds,
capture the vast Panjab within them

It is strange –
on faces, I don't even know
I find the warmth of my grandmother and my mother.
I find myself in these women.
They seem so familiar, like they are my own.

And I see so many stories on each face
waiting to be told,
so many stories covered by dupattas,
stories sitting on the shoulders of so many women,
shoulders that are tired of hiding away cracks and bruises.

But they smile as though nothing has happened.
Their backs and spines hold so much strength
just like my grandmother and mother...

– women back home

****

She puts on her red coloured bangles.
She places a red coloured bindi between her eyes.
Then she lines her young eyes with kohl
and paints her subtle lips red.

She looks at her reflection
in the mirror
and thinks of her childhood days.

She puts on her red coloured salwar kameez,
puts on her golden anklets
and golden earrings and necklace...

For the last time, she looks at her reflection
in the mirror
just before her name is replaced
- her existence completely changed -
like she didn't have an existence before.
From Miss to Mrs
while her going to be husband stays as Mr...

It is like she can simply press ctrl-alt-delete
and delete her entire existence before this day -
her wedding day.

****

Her body must be watched.
The hymen must remain unbroken.

                Look at the way she walks-
                        is she a virgin?
body is not hers
        body is society's
body smells of male chauvinism
body smells of decades of patriarchy
        body is taken away
body is owned
woman told to keep pure
        they whisper
                is she a virgin?
make sure you use white sheets
smell for her blood
look for the sweat on her face

does she scream / or bare the pain
        and while she goes to the bathroom
make sure you check for those blood stains...

****

Hide that your son is infertile,
    blame your daughter-in-law.

Hide your son's sexuality, get him married
and everything will be fine.

Hide it away, no one should know
your husband is cheating on you.
Hide it away; divorce isn't an option
what will society say?

Hide away the doctor's reports; your daughter is fine.
depression doesn't exist in your family.
Your mother died because of heart-attack, nothing major.
Physical health comes first.

Hide away your aspirations.
Get married and have children.
Women in our society can't dream too high.

Hide it away, don't tell anyone your dreams.
log kya kahenge – what will people say.
Keep it hidden. Don't tell anyone. Hide it away.

****

We never really talk about the silence –
that our fathers carry
the way that they carry rivers of emotion
hidden away.

They want to cry, but they don't.
They hide their emotions,
they show anger
when they mean love...

Maybe it is because that is how their father
showed love to their mother...

****

How many more
news headlines of a new rape case?
how many more Nirbhaya's ?
young girls have become living dead bodies
young to old girls... raped.
acid attacks daily
with so many bodies sold daily
girls and women catcalled daily
rape is used sa a weapon of war
politicians use religion to protect their monopoly
fake messiahs draw lines
religion is used as an excuse to kill
temples have become places of rape
God watches over borders placed on women's bodies
how many more rapes?
how many more gang rapes?
God do you exist?
can't you see what is happening?
the world has no humanity left
wars are carried on inside women's bodies
borders are filled with the dead
and some are silenced straight away
and some dead bodies are still penetrated
thousands are raped every second, every day, every day
and no one knows, no one knows...

****

kalam kabhi censored nahi hoti
the pen is never censored.

****

Somewhere centuries ago
before colonists...
somewhere in the pre-Vedic era, my ancestors live
and write poetry deeper than words itself.
The sarees aren't flowing and brown isn't exotic.
        It's a precolonial Bharat.
The Indus flows so beautifully.
        The women show their bare backs
and some walked around naked
reading pages of the Kamasutra.
And some from head to toe are full of gold,
from naths to the payals the gold shines.
        The children sit in the veranda
reading the families of Aryans and Dravidians.
The mothers are cooking and no it's not curry.
It's a blend of so many spices
mixed with so many lentils.
The young girls sit outside
        soaking the rays of the sun
on their golden bodies...

Years, centuries pass by. It's 1857.
Somewhere a young woman awaits her lover.
They send letters to each other.
They meet secretly on the banks of Chenab
but...they come –
and make something pure become impure...
Poison is placed in their mouths.
They are made to hate their tongues.
They try to wash away their accent, but it remains.
All of a sudden a country full of gold

becomes the home of poverty
and the only way for freedom is partition –
the Indus will never see its rivers flow freely
Temples, Gurdwaras and Masjids bid their farewell...
religion becomes the cause of division.
they do what they want...

Many years later, oceans across
and despite colonisation
I live.

****

she awakens look	she awakens look
earth	fire
child	adult
slow	fast
father's daughter	never mother's daughter
love was never a question	choice was already chosen
husband lord	husband lord's
exile and exile	pain and pain
purity	and impurity
character questioned	why?
never thought of vengeance	but vengeance echoed
this world was never hers	a world full of men was never hers
exile ends	silent or outspoken
it never mattered	nights of sin still questioned
no love came forward	no husband lord came
daughter of earth	her saree unfolded and
walks on fire	unfolded
thirsty of pure water	daughter of fire
she returned to her	thirsty of blood

mother earth
no man ever understood
her
Sita

she slipped the slopes of
Himalayas
never to return
Drapuadti

****

dharma, adharma –
virtuous. sin.
what is virtuous?
and what is a sin?
what is right?
and what is wrong?

a virgin sits aside
she, a Brahmin woman
she is said to be pious
for a sinister man
she spends her night
parting her thighs
to the Dalit man

the price of love
equals death

love is the biggest rebellion
it breaks the status quo

razor sharp words
bite tongues
swords kill heads
Manu watches over

Dalit man
she, a Brahmin woman

the price of love
equals death

****

Nudity is not modesty
sex Gods are singing
and people are dying
and before Vatsyayana
Shiva walks across the Himalayas
searching for Parvati...

time changes
but nothing really changes
Krishna comes over and plays his flute
Radha dances...

Silence. Silence. Silence.

Pleasure and spirituality
not to be mixed please.
the silent Buddha weeps
do not break the silent mediation
sex Gods are singing
and people are dying
it's a mix of hell and heaven.

let's burn Raja Ravis paintings
nudity is not modesty

because –
Kama. Artha. Dharma. Moksha.
comes first
and it's a manual, a guide
some tantric sex guide
it's whitewashed love
Khajuraho temples are a lie
Vatsyayana now cries
as his Kamasurta dies.

****

kamasurta ka desh
jaaha kabhi kaam pooja jaata ta
aj apni hi pehchan se bhag raha hai...

the land of the kamasutra
where once sex was worshiped
today is running away from its own identity...

****

Where is my God?
I see so many languages
so many linguistic birds flying
so many that carry ism, schism
but where is my God?

I have been separated from home for so long
that I have forgotten what home looks like
and I've forgotten –
how to speak the language spoken by God

I fall asleep...

and my God dances in my dreams
in yellow and white sarees
half naked playing sitars
drinking the blood of demons
my God comes as Kali Ma and Parvati

my God dances on the spin of the earth's axis
my God comes as Shiva doing the tandava
my God comes as the words of Guru Nanak
the Azaan of the Masjid, the bells of the Church
they all come in my dream
while the Sufi dances to find God

I wake up, and questions are still unanswered
what is the language spoken by God?
what language did God create?
what religion did God create?

I sit trying to find God
trying to listen to the sounds of the universe
within me sits a strange quietness to a raging storm
of an ocean that is endless
questions sit in the ocean never to be solved.

****

blood... boundaries... border...
Guru Nanak transcended borders
so manmade borders are nothing to me.
Panj-aab

home of jogis and fakirs   the home of my Gurus /
home of Sikhs   Hindus   Muslims / split once / split twice
/ Gurmukhi / Shahmukhi / divisions / provinces /
bodies gone. language lost. poets gone.
blood... boundaries... border...
partition is mentioned and I cry.

****

Lost somewhere she is
somewhere before 1966
somewhere before 1947
lost somewhere, maybe between 1799-1849
during her rise

Lost somewhere before –
Bulleh Shah's kalam
Shiv Kumar Batalvi's kitaab
Amrita Pritam's words
before Waris Shah's Heer
lost somewhere maybe between –
the sweet raags and poetry of the 15th century

She's lost somewhere –
maybe at the shore of Chenab
maybe at Takhat Hazara
maybe at Jhang
or maybe, between the valley of mountains

She's lost somewhere –
in pages of history
in pages of literature

in pages of poetry...
and her voice is
lost, lost and lost

Maybe she's somewhere, watching warriors
or somewhere, listening to saints
maybe she's lost somewhere, in the horizon of mustard fields

Maybe she's lost somewhere –
where her five rivers where once together
before her sixth river of blood emerged...

Maybe she's lost between, the borders of Amritsar and Lahore
or lost maybe between, Nankana Sahib and Kartarpur
lost between, Shahmukhi and Gurmukhi maybe

Can someone find her?
does anyone know where she is?
can someone please find my Panjab?
before she gets lost and lost, into pages of history
before this poison of drugs fills her every corner

Can someone please find my Panjab...?
her land that started the academics
with the world's first book – The Rig Veda
today is losing its literature...
please find my Panjab
Bring back my beloved land of warriors, saints, lovers and
poets
Colonists and governments may have divided her
but her soul remains one
undivided –
borders and distance mean nothing when the soul is one

I might be away from my Panjab
but – Panjab is within my heart
and within my soul...

****

> *"I lost my mother at the age three*
> *and at the age of five I lost my mother again*
> *with the partition of Panjab"*

- Deedar Singh Randhawa

****

15th August 1947
while India was celebrating
Panjab was crying
crying tears of blood

Ravi was separated from her sister Chenab
and the river of love became filled with blood

The land that once co-existed with all faiths
today was fighting
Hindu here
Sikh here
Musalman there
no one thought about my Panjab

A line was drawn
and that was it

no one thought about the consequences
the mass migration
the killings
the rapes
the women abducted
the families separated
the houses destroyed

My Lahore, my Nankana
was separated from me
70 years on
I still hear the cries of my people

Panjab was torn apart into two pieces
but – where am I to exist?
when I exist in a united Panjab
a Panjab without Wagah Border
a Panjab where it's five rivers flow together...

****

All lines end one day
          just as cracked lines across the body
          will all end one day

but parallel lines run   across her body
of honour and resilience
her tears hold   mesmerizing waters
she is a Goddess robbed of purity
in the name   of   azaadi

a lost generation of women
a generation that should have lived
died
with human life forgotten

anklets removed   jhumkas taken off
face covered with a dupatta
flesh bleeding through

her sharp tongue of language
holding words of poetry
                die.
yet her dead body is rape/d again and again

and some came forward and silently got beheaded to avoid
being taken away and raped

some on the train didn't have enough time
 to get the bottle of poison out

so the mobs came and sliced their breasts off
they spread salt across and laughed and went

screaming in pain   the name of God   couldn't even be
recited for peace
peace only came   when the bottle of poison was found
some got adducted
and had to married their   own rapist
with no choice but accept to this as their kismat – destiny
so a different name became engraved on the forearm

these boundary lines
made the body of women

warzones and living tombs
with tattoos on genitals...

the next day, eyes closed
she pulls down her salwar
not knowing who is coming
but she dreams of living, of being free... eyes closed

Newspaper headlines stated –
women exchanged must return to their homes
she carries the child of her rapist
with an exchanged name
with an exchanged religion
where will she go?

Some managed to run across the fields,
across rivers to go home
but they weren't welcome anymore
because they've become impure

and   were told to go back where they escaped from...

So many questions unanswered,
and not found in any pages of history –
        why...? why must women's bodies become warzones?
why must innocents suffer?
why? why?

Herstory is history –
        1947 Partition of India

****

It's April Vaisakhi 1919,
and from Lahore to Amritsar
thousands come
everyone gathers, it's so peaceful
        and then,
from old to the young they all got shot
her father dies in front of her own eyes
she ran and ran

It's mid-August 1947,
she is about to get on the train
across to that side, where her own people are
her two-month-old son cries
while her husband gets his sword out
and slices the head off their thirteen-year-old daughter
blood is splattered everywhere
just as they leave their home in Lahore forever

It's early days of a new month - November 1984,
she now lives in Delhi with her family
she is walking slowly while holding her grandson
waiting for her daughter-in-law and son to return home
hours pass by; it's getting late in Delhi
finally, her daughter-in-law comes,
she has blood across her salwar, with her kameez torn
she told her mother-in-law: *he was killed in front of my*
        own eyes
so I ran and ran...

With the remains of her family,
she flees away, oceans across
somewhere unknown...

****

Revolution at Victoria and Albert;
locked away behind glass doors
are items from the East. I stare at art
I stare at paintings of Ranis and Rajas
right now somewhere, someone is dying
someone is dying in flames
and I am staring at art

I think of the brown bodies
and turbans that sit in untold stories
of wwl and ww2
I am trying to write a poem
but no words seem to come. Like my words
have been stolen away

Eyes are covered
with shades of fascism
mixed with colonisation
nazis move over dancing
they don't look at stalin or gandhi
they don't pray to God
but pray for imperialism

Freedom isn't a revolution
it is the rights of every living autonomy
the revolution started back home. I carry
the revolution in my bones
staring at art.

****

Last night I saw God
God was watching me
while I was writing
and I began crying
God came
and said to me – why are you crying?
I said – everything it just hurts, it pains
and I don't have words for the pain this world is
carrying...

God gave me a hug
and told me everything will be okay

I looked at God
and I saw her crying too
I said God – why are you crying?
she said – how can I not, when I am half you...

She – my mother; God

****

young children are dying daily in Syria
Kashmir is bleeding daily
Yemen is crying daily
Panjab is still recovering from the tears of 1947
blood and tears is what is filled the radcliffe line
with the wounds of 1984 fresh in the heart
so much violence so much terror
the Sikh genocide
the Bangladesh genocide
bombs exploding on borders

humans killing humans
Gujarat riots, the Bombay riots
the Holocaust
the Armenian genocide
hidden genocides
Black genocide conspiracy theory
government conspiracies
people are still crying and crying
Yazidis are currently dying
so many mothers are waiting for their children to return
Indigenous people of America
had their homes stripped away
dirty politics are no good
pain is filled everywhere
Iraq, Palestine, Turkey,
Afghanistan, and Pakistan – do I need to say more ...

what do we know of terror?
       ask those whose home is a war zone.

****

Revolution speaks through the waves of Satluj
blood drops are still filling the river
unspoken words by Bhagat Singh, Sukhdev and Rajguru
    float around
Oppression, fascism, tyranny
still exists
with pages of history hungry
Comrades watch away
and pages of Karl Marx fly away

Kartar Singh Sarabha writes away
and the Ghadars leave their conspiracies behind

and beyond borders
beyond capitalist ideals
anti-colonials
anti-imperialists
await for eradication of imperialism
they await to manifest injustice from –
fake governments
fake democracies...

consequences –
lies of freedom
extremism
a corrupt system...
with capitalists writing our own history...

but we must never forget
Inquilab Zindabad
long live the revolution.

****

The rise of fascism
comes in many different forms
and minorities become divided
colours become divided
names become divided
with fake missionaries

religion is used as propaganda
race is used as propaganda
emotions are used as propaganda
the internet doesn't always speak the truth
look. look. look.
read. read. read.

They call it a democracy
while fascism spreads across the west and east
capitalism at its finest
human exploitation at its finest
I don't need to say names
'cause you already know...

Immigrants cry over
brown and black skin watch over
sex trafficking and religion
is stuck in between
while refugees get raped
borders filled with blood
truth shouts away
lies cover it away
but truth comes forward...

The rise of fascism
comes in many different forms
in many different forms...

****

Closed orders, closed laws
behind closed doors, no one knows

no one knows,
that there is a parrot in a cage
while the radio plays
it repeats – another bomb
and another rape
human rights move over
closed files on desks
baby activists speak up for a day
soon they get tired
but the parrot in the cage
repeats – another bomb
and another rape
Rome was built on ruins
so maybe the rest of world can too –
be rebuilt and hide the deeds
I wanted to place my hand across the globe
and shout the words **PEACE** –
but the parrot in the cage
repeats – another bomb
and another rape
where if I wanted to
could I place my hands? –
and say human rights are rights
and that across borders there is no hate and pain
that humans are not being dragged and killed
rape is not being used as a weapon of war
that hate doesn't fill borders. that blood doesn't fill border lines.
the parrot in the cage
repeats – *another bomb*
and another rape

****

I dream of a place
I dream of a Kashmir
that could be free
I dream of peace
I dream of a Panjab
that doesn't exist
In my dream, I see no border
I see Lahore and Amritsar side by side
I dream of a place
I dream of a Kabul
that could be free
that could be what it was
before this blood
before this terror existed
I dream of a place
I dream of Syria
where children play
and not get killed
I dream of a place
I dream of an earth
where humans exist with humanity
I dream of a place
where there is love
and where there is co-existence

I dream
and
I dream...

****

Don't wish to be a kavi, a poet
you'll turn pain to poetry
and that becomes addictive

The word kavi comes from Sanskrit origin
from a root kū meaning to cry out
maybe that is why when you read a poets work
you can hear their soul crying.

****

meri rooh da qaraar mera Panjab
my souls tranquillity is my Panjab.

****

Jhelum
the verses from religious scriptures
so holy. holy. holy
but blood spills and ink spills
and hidden away are the scriptures
along children under beds
and I pray. I pray. I pray.

Chenab
the epitome of love filled with tragedy
you couldn't save Sohni
your waters consumed her
Heer first saw her Ranjha in your open arms
and she consumed poison in your closed arms

many lovers came and went
but none like the lovers
that existed before 1947.

Ravi
you remind me of my mother
you remind me of her long flowing hair
you remind me of Sita
you remind me of resilience
you remind me of power.

Beas
flowing from the crown
coming from the tikka of Hind
from the horizon of the Himalayas
qawwalis sing in the air
and the bulbul sings along
katiya karoon tera roon
katiya karoon tera roon
I will spin your cotton
I will spin your cotton.

Satluj
they say Kasur is still silent
but they say you can still hear Bulleh Shah
they say you can still see him dancing
and they say you can hear the soul of Bhagat Singh crying
with history lying.

Panjnad
when soul parts body
the body dies
but the soul lives on

the five
the five rivers flow
and you come alive
flowing through the Indus
the Mirasis sing away
mixing Panjabi from Majha, Malwa and Doaba
with Mirpuri, Sindhi and Seraiki
all accents and languages mix
flowing from the five rivers
through the seven seas
to the rest of the world.

****

The birds are singing super early
with Gurdwareh speakers going off at 5 a.m
it's Chet it's a new year
coming faster year after year
reflections of the past
with a chance to start again

colours of blue and orange
Vaisakh comes with flowers blossoming
the fields of mustards are glowing
warriors and saints pass by
with folklore coming natural

and the phulkariyan are flying
dancing in the rain
with mehndi hands swinging on swings
gidha time across the fields
it's the month of Saun

having kheer with malpure
cold lassi and sometimes fresh ganna juice

Patjhad for a while
the cold nights of Poh
spent around fire reading poetry
Bhagat Singh and Udham Singh
watching from above
looking at the manmade border
east and west Panjab
united through poetry....
with some saag
and makki di roti/

Phaggan comes and it is time to fall in love once again...

****

tere saaha vich mera saah muk jaave
eh mera akhari saah hove

in your breath may my breath finish
may this be my last breath

****

Love isn't a word
that is captured within
          a certain language...
but when you ask me about love

I don't quite know
how to explain it
as in my mother tongue
there isn't just one word
   there are so many words
words which get lost in translation
to one word
to one meaning
love.

ishq, pyar, prem, mobhabat, preet...
– love.
              love is when the soul breaks
the cage of words
   so love happens,
and ink touches paper   love happens

love is not always poetry
sometimes poetry is love
sometimes the poem looks like a new love
sometimes the poem looks just like love

love is the sound of rain
while reading
and love is your voice
your voice is poetry in motion
love is what I do
all over your skin   leaving poetry

love happens when I dance like a Sufi
singing ghazals
thinking I am dervish in love
writing poetry

love happens
when you touch my skin   leaving perfect calligraphy scripts
in different languages of love

love is not translated words
love is pure
love is real

                  more than poetry

They ask me of love –
when it can't be defined...

Love is spoken through the eyes.
    love is something that you feel
love breaks the mirror of the soul
love soothes the heart –
    writing pages of poetry
in a language lost in translation...

****

Five rivers flow
in my soul –
       the rivers across oceans
flow into my soul

I close my eyes
and remember
     my last night
my night
spent in your arms
       at Noor Mahal

drinking poetry into midnight
sometimes reading the verses of Shiv Kumar Batalvi
and sometimes Waris Shah...

In the blanket of twilight
it was just you and I
       and hung up in the sky
was the moon
with its light shining through your body

And then, the sun came
through the domes of the Mahal
and melted in your eyes
I felt like, maybe I was Heer
and maybe you –
my Ranjha...

****

Sometimes I want to complain
par tum toh mere ho nahi
toh shikaat kaise karo –
but you are not mine
then how can I complain?

agar main, main nah hoti
aur tum, tum nah hotey
if I wasn't me
and you wasn't you
who knows maybe we wouldn't meet as strangers...
and maybe you wouldn't be my unknown love/r....

****

We sang love songs in our mother tongues
while looking at each other
and drinking Rooh-afza
to nourish our rooh

Forever catching trains, changing cities
to make love far away
going to places where no one knows who I am...

and just like Mirza Sahiban
I wanted us to become rebels of love
becoming proper ishaqzaade
but love is meant to be paak, paakeeza – pure
with no physical intimacy they say...

That night while you fell asleep in my arms
I stole the blackness of the night sky
into the ink of my pen
to write a poem about you
I spent the night writing
while you slept away
the morning came and the sun rose....
my eyes opened and I smiled.

and I went away... once again...
dreaming of
catching trains to change cities
to drink Rooh-afza
to sit by your side
and read away the lines of Batalvi–
ikk kudi jeeda naam mohabbat
ghum hai, ghum hai, ghum hai

a girl, whose name is love,
is missing, is missing, ah, missing.

****

I want to dance like Bulleh Shah
and write you a kalma in ishq

I want to write you a ghazal like Ghalib
filled with cinnamon and ishq

I want to give you my everything
just like how Mansoor did in ishq

I want to swim across the river Chenab
just like Sohni and drown in your ishq

I want to be the fragrance
that comes towards you as ishq

and finally, I want to become ishq
I want to become your ishq.

****

You look like a poem that Rumi would write
completed by Ghalib
with a few words from Bulleh Shah maybe
I wonder why you seem so familiar
like it was always meant to be – you and me

From the sun setting to the sun rising
to the birds singing
to the Azaan of the Masjid
to the bells of the Church
in the words of Gurbani
to the prayers of Krishna
to the Himalayas
and across the seven seas
there is love everywhere...

now, I hear you in all
and I see you in all
in the arch of Mandir
in the pillars of a Masjid
I see you
and my soul and my body lingers of you
lingers of your fragrance

This love isn't from today
it isn't one of rajas and ranis
this love is older than the tales of Yusuf and Zulaikha
this love is older than Shiv and Shakti
this love is more than love
this love is freedom
this love is azaadi
this love is mine and yours only –
a tale from the beginning of time right to the end.

And this love will never die
when my soul parts my body
it won't be the end
my ash will dissolve into the earth that was made from love

I will dissolve in love
and my soul will merge into you
and become love forever and ever
I will truly become love
I will truly become you
because I realise now –
it was meant to be
only me and you
no one else
just me and you
and it will be and you
forever until the end of time...

****

I lost a ghazal; I lost a ghazal
I think I left at your doorstep...

It's been awhile since I last saw you
It's been awhile since your lips touched mine

Like a dancing Sufi, we danced and danced
we became one, under the ecstasy of ishq

That night, I lost a ghazal
I lost the words and the sweetness

I became the wandering Sufi
I became the Sufi in your ishq

My lips are still dripping with your taste,
and I still haven't found my ghazal...

But I will wander in your ishq, and I will find the ghazal
which I left at your doorstep, inside me.

****

apne dil ko bana kar kitaab-e-izhaar
tere naam ki siyahi se likh di iqraar-e-mohabbat

i made my heart the book of expression
with the ink of your name i wrote the confession of love

****

your one hand in mine
and your other hand flicking through
the Diwan of Ghalib
taking us to purani Dilli, old Dilli
to mughliyah mahals
and the aadha of umrao jaan came alive
with ghazals echoing high in high walls

we started to walk through the streets of Dilli
and Urdu fuses with Hindi

each corner seems to be saying
Dilli is Ghalib
and Ghalib is Dilli...

we reach the end of the street
and the dark night
hides us away
we are just one kiss away,
one touch away and
and the wind blew the pages of the Diwan....

mohabbat mein nahin hai farq jeene aur marne ka,
usi ko dekh kar jeete hain, jis kaafir pe dam nikle...

when in love, there is little difference between life and death,
the same infidel is my life, for whom I could give my last breath...

****

If I confess my love to you
please do not compare my love –
to the love of Sassi, Sohni, Sahiban or Heer
because if you do... then I have already failed...
in this baazi of ishq.

****

And maybe one day
I'll take you to my Panjab
which is divided by rivers but not soul

Maybe one day
I'll take you to Takhat Hazara
and you'll become my Ranjha
and I'll become your Heer

Maybe one day
I'll take you to the shore of Chenab
and our love will blossom like Sohni-Mahiwal

Maybe one day
I'll read you Shiv Kumar Batalvi
whose poetry soothes my soul

Maybe one day
I'll read you Bulleh Shah's kalam
whose poetry runs through my every pore

Maybe one day
I'll read you Amrita Pritam's poetry
who made Waris Shah alive once again

Maybe one day
I'll learn how to flow my ink strokes into
Shahmukhi
just like Gurmukhi

Maybe one day
I'll take you to Nankana Sahib by Lahore
where Guru Nanak was born

Maybe one day
I'll take you to Khair-ud-din Masjid in Amritsar

And maybe one day
I'll take you to my Panjab
which is divided by rivers but not soul...

****

everyone looks at your rUp – face
hardly anyone looks at your rUh – soul...

    – roop and rooh, only one letters difference;

    one letter that changes everything.

ACKNOWLEDGEMENTS

Above all, God thank you.

Thank you Stuart for believing in me. If it wasn't for you and Amerah, Rooh would have never happened.

My grandparents my ancestors this is for you but mostly this book is for my mother who I am nothing without, the poetry comes from her. My father and my brother who show me the world in the different light.

My best friends– Shanice, Niharika, Hamida, Demi and Amrit so much love for you all.

A big thank you to my friends Amrita and Tanya for that whats app convo that got me writing poetry love you both.

Harmanjit thank you the most for persuading me to perform at the Nishaan open mic back in 2o16 that led me to a whole different world.

Thank you to all the amazing poets and creative peeps I've met along my journey you've all inspired me in some way.

My social media fam lots of love to you all.

And you dear reader thank you.

And most importantly thank you poetry for being my saviour.

ABOUT VERVE POETRY PRESS

Verve Poetry Press is a new press focussing initially on meeting a local need in Birmingham - a need for the vibrant poetry scene here in Brum to find a way to present itself to the poetry world via publication. Co-founded by Stuart Bartholomew and Amerah Saleh, it will be publishing poets this year from all corners of the city - poets that represent the city's varied and energetic qualities and will communicate its many poetic stories.

As well as this wonderful collection from Rupinder - look out in 2018 for stunning first collections from Amerah, Casey Bailey Leon Priestnall, Nafeesa Hamid, Kamil Mahmood and Hannah Swings, to name but a few. And watch this new press bring the colour and attitude of Verve Poetry Festival, our sister in Birmingham based poetry activity, to all its publishing and event-making.

Like the festival, we will strive to think about poetry in inclusive ways and embrace the multiplicity of approaches towards this glorious art.

So watch this space. Verve Poetry Press has arrived!

www.vervepoetrypress.com
@VervePoetryPres
mail@vervepoetrypress.com